# wild and still

# Praise for *Wild and Still*

Maryann Russo's wise and gentle poems weave an intimate landscape in which small and daily moments—a butterfly's amble, pressed white shirts, an old pen, a field of tulips, a walk on the beach, a hummingbird—become mirrors for a seeking spirit. Her words take the reader on a sensual journey of discovery back to the center, to that sweet place in the soul, which is, as the poet notes, both wild and still.
—**Deborah Edler Brown, Author of** *Red Long Hot Peppers,* *Haiku Volcano,* **and** *Grandparents as Parents: A Survival Guide for Raising a Second Family*

*Wild and Still* celebrates that seemingly small space that connects the physical and spiritual world.
Russo's words quietly take us into the larger world.
—**Susan B. Gilbert, Author of** *Blue White Veil*

Maryann Russo's work offers us a stay in the garden among the lush dahlias and pomegranates of her words.
Here are poems which trace her evolution from "a childhood of lines" to a maturity of music which will entice and sustain the reader.
—**Alison Luterman, Author of** *The Largest Possible Life* **and** *See How We Almost Fly*

Maryann Russo's carefully crafted poems remind us that we are not enough in the worlds of nature and poetry, and that in order to travel there, we must, along with the poet, "release [our] penchant for exactitude".
—**Jeanetta Calhoun Mish, Author of** *Work Is Love Made Visible* **and editor of Women Writing Nature: A Special Edition of Sugar Mule Literary Magazine**

Maryann Russo's poetry will flower within you, bringing forth a translucent energy and wisdom. Like the "certain bees" in her poem "Unfolding," you will be called to a "center," and taken on a small but important journey into the wild stillness of that center.

**—Sakada, Author of *Into a Long Curl***

Russo's collection, *Wild and Still*, possess a wonderfully meditative quality that draws the reader into a quiet place where the ideas of being light, of flying, of being winged and therefore free in some way, pursue the speaker. She negotiates beautifully the questions and stories of the past—being free from them—and the coming to terms with the truth of them.

**—Colette Speer, Author of *Mean* (published under her former name, Colette LaBouff Atkinson)**

*"We shall not cease from exploration
And the end of our exploring
Will be to arrive where we started
And know the place for the first time."*

**—T.S. Eliot**

# wild and still

**POEMS**
## Maryann Russo

Inspiration Pointe Press

Published by Inspiration Pointe Press,
an imprint of
Over and Above Creative Group, Los Angeles, CA
www.overandabovecreative.com

Copyright © 2013 by Maryann Russo. All rights reserved.
ISBN 978-0-9890917-0-1
Library of Congress Control Number: 2016914029

This book contains material protected under International and Federal Copyright Laws and Treaties. No part of this publication may be reproduced, distributed, or transmitted in any form or by any means, including photocopying, recording, or other electronic or mechanical methods, without the prior written permission of the author, except in the case of brief quotations embodied in critical reviews and certain other noncommercial uses permitted by copyright law.

For permission requests, please email the publisher at following address: s.shankin@overandabovecreative.com.

Designed by Susan Shankin
Cover photo by Desislava Vasileva
Author photo by Kristen Hastings

Visit Maryann at www.Facebook.com/MaryannRussoAuthor

If you enjoyed reading this book,
we appreciate your review of it on Amazon
and on other book review websites.

# acknowledgments

My first thanks now and always must go to Sister Laurentia, my college English professor and early mentor for whom my computer is named.

When I was nineteen, unbeknownst to me, she submitted my sonnet to *The Atlantic Monthly*, where it won a Merit Award. She taught me to sit with a blade of grass for an hour and just write. She helped me fall in love with poetry.

I am grateful to Christine Leigh and the Wild Women Writers who fostered my writing for years.

I am also thankful to Sakada, a Los Angeles poet and teacher, who taught me so much, especially how to get out of the way of my own words, and to the original FYG WYG's Susan Gilbert and Elgee Tavanlar-Amato, for our amazing Saturday workshops.

Thanks to Kathryn Sandow for our many meetings for the sake of our words.

I am deeply grateful for poet Deborah Edler Brown, my current mentor and guide. Her ongoing permission to be the poet only I can be, to allow my words outside the box, continues to grow my work.

I wish to thank *Lunarosity* and *Sugar Mule* for first publishing some of the poems in this book.

I also extend my profound gratitude to *poeticdiversity* for nominating me for the Pushcart Prize and for inviting me to become a Contributing Editor to their publication.

I want to acknowledge my dear friends Olivia LaBouff, Barbara Joseph and CB Schultz for being my readers and cheerleaders.

Thanks to my siblings, Ron, John and Theresa, for being my life-long friends and witnesses.

Thank you to my daughter Anne, and my husband Mike, for your steadfast support and enthusiasm.

Thank you to my publishers Susan Shankin and Rick Benzel at Over and Above Creative Group for helping me to be just that.

And finally thank you to each one who has been a part of the fabric of my life, and therefore my poetry.

## contents

| | |
|---|---|
| *Creation* | 1 |
| *The Garden* | 2 |
| *April 2, 1951* | 3 |
| *Heart-sleeve* | 4 |
| *Instead* | 5 |
| *The Heresy of Lines* | 6 |
| *In Words* | 8 |
| *My Father's Pens* | 9 |
| *not too many words, please* | 11 |
| *Rapprochement* | 12 |
| *Not Just a Walk on the Beach* | 13 |
| *Unfolding* | 15 |
| *Voice* | 16 |
| *Salsa* | 17 |
| *Tales* | 18 |
| *Q & A* | 19 |
| *Egress* | 20 |
| *Morning* | 21 |
| *Tulips* | 22 |

| | |
|---|---|
| *Moses Re-imagined* | 23 |
| *Allowing* | 24 |
| *Time-lapse* | 25 |
| *Morning Glories in Big Sur* | 26 |
| *The Center of Things* | 27 |
| *Open* | 28 |
| *After the Rain* | 29 |
| *Bi-Polar Ocean* | 31 |
| *Near* | 32 |
| *Regina* | 33 |
| *Camouflage* | 34 |
| *Gladiolas* | 35 |
| *Invitation* | 36 |
| *Enough* | 37 |
| *Unleashed* | 38 |
| *How to Bite Into a Verb Sandwich* | 39 |
| *At Last* | 40 |
| *Koloiki Ridge Hike* | 41 |
| *Peace Lily* | 42 |
| *Beyond Measure* | 43 |
| *Birds Know* | 44 |

| | |
|---|---|
| *One White Slipper* | *45* |
| *Swan* | *46* |
| *Carried* | *47* |
| *What a Sea Can Hold* | *48* |
| *The Mindfulness of Birds* | *49* |
| *Still Life* | *50* |
| *Grace* | *51* |
| *Without Words* | *52* |
| *Trinity* | *53* |
| *Hummingbird* | *54* |
| *Without Conclusion* | *55* |
| *Hope Afloat* | *56* |
| *A Discarded Tendril* | *57* |
| *Liberty* | *58* |
| *Stealing Home* | *59* |
| *Hide and Seek* | *60* |
| *The Offering* | *61* |
| *Home* | *62* |
| *Here* | *63* |
| *Dance* | *64* |
| *About the Author* | *65* |

## *Creation*

It is in the noiseless abyss
that everything is born.

It is in the soundless place
that I can actually hear

and then they come,

    one at first
    followed by more

    innocent and delicious.

"In the beginning was the word ... "

So I begin.

## *The Garden*

We were in the garden
overgrown green
flush with magnolia and dahlia
wide and fragrant
invited to slide down their stems
into their centers

We heard the songs of exotic birds
though we did not see them
caught the quick flap of wings
and glimpsed the leaves tipping over
after they launched

We were in that garden
the one with peaches and pomegranates
but we wanted the mangos
plush ruby fruit
ripe on their branches
calling

We ate
swallowed our innocence
and suddenly
naked

fled

## *April 2, 1951*

In the photo
my five-year-old eyes
squint with delight.

My hands grasp
a glass plate
which holds my
birthday cake.

Mother kneels beside me,
hair swept from her forehead,
fifties style, a silk scarf tied
loosely around her neck.
Light brown curls
touching her shoulders.

Her eyes are green and clear,
not yet red from the alcohol
that would douse her secrets
and wash her away.

She smiles past me,
I cannot tell where.
To the geraniums just blooming?
Some childhood memory
of her own?

I lift the plate
as if it were an offering
to the sun-lit sky.

## *Heart-sleeve*

My mother accused me
of wearing my heart
on my sleeve.

How could my heart
wander
from its hidden center

and make its way
to my sleeve,
dangling

susceptible
to any breeze
that could carry it away?

## *Instead*

I could have spent my time
immersed in one butterfly's
amble across the sidewalk
on gossamer legs,
wings spread.

Instead, I stride
through my front door
scan the white moldings,
vigilant for dust,
and wipe them clean.

I could have stopped
to watch her lift,
then flit in her fickle way
blossom to blossom
until she landed
nuzzle-deep in the center
of a fragrant flower.

Instead,
I rinse my hands,
and return to the next
order of business.

## *The Heresy of Lines*

My childhood was a lined existence;
my first-grade picture shows a girl
with hedged brown bangs.

By age ten I was required
to iron my father's shirts,
pressing crisp lined creases
down long white sleeves.

In school, the nuns kept us in straight lines
for flag salute and assemblies.
Our desks were placed precisely
on edges of linoleum squares
that formed perfect lines.

For homework, I composed,
memorized, and recited lines.
Shame accompanied crayon marks
that strayed across.

Today, I hereby release
my penchant for exactitude,
here on unlined paper
in uneven verse.

I promise to see
between the lines,
under the lines,
beyond the lines.

I will respect whatever
is wrinkled, wadded,
scrunched, curved,

meandering

I will allow my mind to leap
like an uncaged cat onto
warm green drenched grasses.

I will scatter seeds
knowing they will
find their own ways to blossom

unexpected

random

wild.

## *In Words*

We meet in words —

written or etched
into the base of a statue

flung harshly
settling in the marrow
breaking our bones

whispered kindly
smoothing the splintered edges

We meet in words —

unspoken yet heard
in the silent corridors of touch

waiting to tell
hiding at the end of the line
afraid to step up

words to declare a thaw —
to make room for the river

## My Father's Pens

I write with one of my father's pens.
That's got to be good luck.
His father was a 16-year-old immigrant
playing the clarinet
from Italy
to Ellis Island.

My father wrote poems and lyrics
that never left their pages
to become music.

The pens he ordered by the dozens.
This one is black with a pink tip,
his old address on Fiesta Green and
phone number printed along with his name.

He carried a handful in his top shirt pocket
wherever he went,
and gave them away
to attractive bank tellers and market clerks.

Now, I hold his pen—
from his pocket—
to write words that will lift
beyond the page

to say somehow
I am happy to be here
in this place
with his name
and fingers like his,

a heart with secrets
like birds
now ready
to lift from their nests.

## *not too many words, please*

    (after Mary Oliver)

words are all around me
sometimes they shout
stop look listen
see me
don't see me

sometimes they sing
as if on a street corner
performing

often they line up
hoping to be chosen

I long for the lapses
when my words are caught off guard
stunned, naked
dancing and transparent

## *Rapprochement*

I still long to venture from the safety
of what I think I know
to the release of my grasp,
palms open,

a heart held
in its commitment to contract
and expand
until it stops.

Oh the coming and going
from the center of things –
knowing there is comfort near,
a vast universe to explore

knowing there is nothing
but unknowing
to wrap around
the clear sharp points
of arrival and
departure.

## Not Just a Walk on the Beach

### I

A butterfly, lemon-yellow,
trimmed with black splotches,
beats its significant wings,
landing and lifting
off tiny tufts
of white petals.

### II

Her thin limbs
coil and tangle
in a wheel chair,
while an attendant
pushes the chair
with one hand.

Dark brown bangs
cover her eyes as she
slumps in the seat,
her mouth gaping,
her face beaming.

### III

In the front seat
of a sedan parked
along the esplanade,
a man moves his mouth
quickly into his cell phone.

In the back, a tow-headed toddler
sits strapped in the car seat;
his azure eyes glazed,
as he stares through the window.

### IV

A mother strolls tall,
one hand around the belly
of her red-headed baby
nestled in a halter.

The other hand holds
a small lime-green umbrella,
shading her daughter's fair skin.

Her baby wears the
smug smile of a girl
who does not yet doubt
her security.

### V

He is tan and toothless,
grinning and reeking
of weed.

As he begs for spare change,
he hoists a large plastic bottle,
slurring, "I only drink water."

I give him two dollars,
touching his hand slightly.

### VI

As I near home,
the butterfly invites a question:

How does one move
   from a stifled furl,
     into a spacious span
        of waiting sky?

## *Unfolding*

I feel wet winged
and wrapped,
dark and tight.

I wonder if
a rose bud
feels similar,
still swaddled
in her womb
of petals —

knowing she is
barely ripe
not ready
to expose herself

yet still emitting
her own perfume,
calling certain bees
to her center.

## *Voice*

she must step out of the script

her voice
will be the feet that move her
the wings that fly
through the heart-portals

with tongue and breath
   words
      give flight

and the steady beat
  of truth
    alights
  on the waiting trees

## *Salsa*

The red tip of her thin white stick
leads four steps down
from the door of her dingy apartment,
then sixty-four steps
to the bus stop.

Along the way she catches the scent
of urine and hears a homeless man
wash his face in the fountain.

She counts three steps on to the bus
and rides twenty minutes across town.
Then she taps her stick back and forth,
back and forth,
prodding the pavement
until she reaches the community center.

Inside the door
fifteen others crowd the room.
The leader turns the boom box on.

She sets her cane
carefully on the bench
and begins to move her hips.

She sways and smiles

as if no one is watching.

## *Tales*

I told stories
over time
woven from old wounds
and the plots of last night's dreams

the gossamer threads
became strong
and complex
my designs
glistened in
the first light
of day

and I carried what got stuck
in those threads

and I believed
what I saw
captive in the silk frames

until
a word
or a touch
broke through
the webbed walls
of my
creation

and the old folds
of my stories
fell

my wings set free
to fly

# Q & A

How can I learn to swim?

> Dive deep into the ocean.
> Your arms will become fins.

How can I learn to fly?

> Walk to the cliff's edge.
> Jump.
> Your arms will grow wings.

How will I find the sky and the sea?

> With wing and fin,
> glide and float
> in the expanse
> that holds you

## *Egress*

Any crack
can be a portal

A fissure in concrete
brings green
pushing through

The slit
between two blinds
invites light

A millisecond
between thoughts
allows
truth
to slip in
like an
unwanted guest

## *Morning*

The night gropes about
lost in its shadows,
waiting for a dawn
that will rescue it.

Day does not slip
into its new world
fresh and ready
to relieve the watch.

No—day must break—
shattering the darkness
with one shard of light
cracking open the night.

## *Tulips*

We light this field
with vibrant
yellow, red-orange
raspberry,

our lucent petals
like cups
drink in the sun,
susceptible to
any wind
or footfall.

We watch
the fast clip
of your walk,
mind-heavy.

We flirt with you,
standing rod-straight
with a slight sway,
exposing our fragile
centers.

How would it be if you
stopped

rested
on this greening
ground
looked up,
one with us

allowed your
own translucence?

## *Moses Re-imagined*

*"Out beyond thoughts of right doing
and wrong doing, there is a field.
I will meet you there."* — Rumi

>He hoists
>the massive tablets
>well above his head,
>his camel slipping
>down the precarious slopes
>of Mount Tabor,
>
>all the thou-shalt-nots
>dodged like
>boulders ready to
>crush any hopes of heaven.
>
>Finally reaching
>the bottom,
>he drops the stones,
>etched with rules,
>weighty and wordy.
>
>See him
>clean-shaven
>striding bare-backed
>out of that desert
>(forty years was long enough).
>
>Hear the first splash
>of hooves into the stream
>wet and edged with green.

# *Allowing*

the space
between
words

the pause
between
breaths

a slit in concrete
steam rising from hot coffee
the silence
of the split second
before the wave recedes
into its ocean

## *Time-lapse*

Not sixty minutes
after the just-cut bud,
blood-red and folded,
was placed in a vase,

its first petal
    dropped —

a lip lowered,
the bottom lip,
    agape,

providing the
opening
for all manner
of things.

## *Morning Glories in Big Sur*

The morning glories
are pale pink and
soft white,
tiny trumpets
with a song:

> It takes only
> a hint of light
> through thick fog
>
> for our faces
> to unfurl.

## *The Center of Things*

A paleontologist
cracked the fossil
of a 38 million year old
tyrannosaurus rex

After all these eons
soft tissue emerged
evidence of blood vessels
sticky, malleable
not the expected
crumble of stone

Within us
there lives
a softness
though we guard it
with layers

though we think
we can harden
our hearts
to keep from
breaking
open

lest
we expose
the soft centers
that have always been

## *Open*

What will fill the wide hole
of my motherless heart
now that I have forgiven you?

You made your way with cigarettes,
vodka and soap operas
trying to soothe yourself.

You taught me to navigate a small world,
to tread my waters,
not dare to swim.

You did the best you could.

Who can I be
now that I have
clipped the strings of blame

rendering my heart
    open?

## *After the Rain*

### I

You huddle
in your blanket,
soft black cotton
red trim,

and bristle
at any threat
of light —

hoping for
another day
dark and wet.

### II

You were only eight
when I left
your father and you
in our small house.

Too soon
a second husband
shared my bed

Your skies
became troubled —
dense clouds gathered,

and your sun-lit
chapters
closed.

### III
Darkness continues
to draw you in.

You still finger
the satin edges of
your blanket.

### IV
I know my part in this.

### V
Look—

the after-the-rain air
clarifies
the white crests
of distant mountains

and carries
the black tipped
wings of gulls

without effort.

Come.

See.

## *Bi-Polar Ocean*

You do not fool me
this morning
all meek,
your waves
barely lapping to shore,
your surface flat and grey

tomorrow you could
arise,
crashing
like a crowd of
dissonant cymbals
loudly pronouncing
yourself

I cannot count
on your moods
or know for sure
which part of you
will show up

you are disparate
unpredictable

passionate
to your core

I would not
change you
if I could

# *Near*

The butterfly grove
is nearer than you think
thick and breezy

inside my thoughts
frail white wings
appear
and disappear

There is music here
listen for the brush of wings
and pulsating hearts

spending every last beat
just to be near the flowers

## *Regina*

Blonde dreadlocks
skim her shoulders
An indigo skirt
brushes mahogany calves
Her coral halter
exposes the ruby stud in her navel

Bare feet pad the sand
in rhythmic steps
first toward the shore
then away

Hips sway in wide
easy circles
She and the ocean
are locked in their dance

Arms move to the beat
of feet as she pumps
toward the waves

to feel the kiss
of the white foam
on her toes

## *Camouflage*

A cacophony of squawking
shatters the morning silence.

A crowd of emerald green parrots
erupts from the leaves of a tall palm tree.

As birds disperse
the only sound is a fury of wings.

## *Gladiolas*

The gladiolas love to surprise,
standing tall and straight
with no peeks
of their budding
for days.

Suddenly, they plume into brilliance,
burst onto the scene
strutting their stuff
all scarlet and blossom

glowing for all they are worth.

## *Invitation*

Wade through the thick
separation of leaves
to find the flower,
flirting outrageously,
swaying her petals
like full hips
swirling beneath a tiny waist.

Honey-yellow nectar calls:

> come—get close
> smell my sweetness.
> get so close
> your lips brush
> the golden stamen tips.

Now enter

## *Enough*

This giant monarch
is drunk from her
last petal-binge.

Her orange wings,
laced with black,
teeter on the ground
which edges the garden.

She readies to rest
near this lilac grove —

where she had opened and
closed her wide wings
to alight on the centers of the
just-opened buds,

where it is enough
to spend her short life
swooning and fluttering
amongst the flowers.

## *Unleashed*

check out the unleashed life
all a scamper and a twitter
tromp through dirt
leading with your forefeet
and the back will follow

there is no need for a watch
bound and buckled
around your wrist
like a weight
numbers to direct you
in endless circles

there are no increments
carefully measured
and doled
no calories

counting disappears
there are too many planets
and stars and moons
let them stud the expanse

all lives emerge
and diverge
a dance
of comings and
goings
one pulse
deep
beats in us all

## *How to Bite Into a Verb Sandwich*

The directions are in the question
Just bite
and be ready
to sink into the layers of doing
planting and growing
chopping and slicing
spreading and placing

from seed to tomato
from turkey to slice
from milk to cheese

Your incisors cut through the perfect design
meant to crumble
meant to swallow
and become
what feeds you

no longer recognizable
as sandwich or verb

## *At Last*

I let go of the dry banks,
    earth slipping through my fingers
    as I slide
    out of the hardened clay of my mind

over and over
    yes

allowing the current
to take me
cool and crisp
rolling, tumbling
    into the river's heart

## *Koloiki Ridge Hike*

If you were here
you would hear the stillness
of thick green cliffs
and revel at the white wings of a single bird
gliding in the corridors
of the gully

If you were here
the Kukui groves would bow
with the slight silence of their leaves
in the island breezes
and the sisal plants
which line the trail
would open to you

just as you are

even with your worry
that neither gratitude
nor the present moment
can hold you
as this red earth holds
the thin stalks
of the Cooke pines

though you are
as wary as the Axis Deer
that roam and disappear
into the forest
with the mere rustle
of a foot on the path

## *Peace Lily*

a variegated leaf
emerges from
the dark earth

a dancer
twirling tall
and tight
her thin legs
planted

her folded hands
raised in prayer

she offers herself

## *Beyond Measure*

We can know how high
a mountain stands
but this says nothing of the breadth
and crumble of the earth rising
and falling
to form the mountain
and the life hidden in its crevices
wild and stalking

No measure can speak
to the patience of grass
    now sprouting
    now green
    now brown
    now gone

No measure can reveal
the beauty that the
stars have seen

or humans
even from their distance

## *Birds Know*

Birds know
when the sun is about to set
they stop whatever they are doing

some gather
their small bodies
to bob on the waves
finding warmth on the water

others wing toward them
swooping to settle in

a final few quicken
their flight to join
with awkward landings
this convergence

of wings and water
of sun and clouds
the last bursts of light
spilling a path onto the sea

they linger
in the lull
of the dark waters

## *One White Slipper*

(after Mary Oliver)

The moon is a white slipper
hanging over the night ocean.
I cannot imagine the fathoms of miles
between this sliver
and the dark waters

Yet the cast of light
is unmistakable
like a blessing
on the patch of sea below

I want to cast light
without knowing it
without trying
as I go about my ways
wearing one white slipper

leaving the rest to the sky.

## *Swan*

Who would call this a swan
lanking its web-footed way
across the dirt
looking for all its worth
lost and clumsy
until it bends on
spindly legs
slides into the lake
where it at long last
belongs
preening and gliding
its white winged way
across the water

## *Carried*

what is a leaf to do
once fallen

but to be carried
by the breeze
that sweeps it

by the ripples of the lake
not even the fish can see

## *What a Sea Can Hold*

This bottle cap
battered but intact
drifted from Carpenteria

That patch of tar
spewed from a tanker
off San Pedro

A seaweed cluster
floats along the coast
from Sausalito

This slim feather
fell from the body
of a wounded gull

> and these ashes
> were released
> from the bow of a boat
> or the edge of a sheer cliff
> or a pier's railing
> at sunset
>
> released from the palms
> of mourners
> in their rituals
>
> who believe
> through their tears that
> the sea can hold it all

## *The Mindfulness of Birds*

A diversity of gulls
black, white, brown
mottled,
convenes on the sand.

They stand gazing
in the same direction,
mesmerized by
the ocean's steady hum.

They are so focused.
My intrusion on the tracks
which run through their caucus
causes only a silent parting

making way for me
without ruckus
without ever turning their faces
away from the sea.

## *Still Life*

One golden pear sits
primly on its bottom
atop a square wooden board.
A bottle of wine stands straight,
next to a wide rimmed glass
half-filled with burgundy.
A wedge of camembert cheese
poses by the glass.
A single red rose reclines on the table.

See the bottle, lip uncorked,
a few blood-like drops
glistening on the cutting board.
Look, a bruised pear lies on its side
split in half, spilling seeds.
The tip of the cheese is rugged,
point gone with one hasty bite.
Several rose petals are scattered
across the table.

Life, unstilled.

## *Grace*

Whole wheat and white cheddar,
fresh salsa and guacamole.
I order this quesadilla
three times a week.

I see the hands that knead
and flatten the tortillas,
pluck tomatoes from their vines,
hold the knife
and chop them finely.

I feel the hands
that drop seeds into the furrowed earth,
pull the cow's udders,
and mill the wheat.

Before I lift the first wedge
I bow my head.

My hands join
with theirs.

## *Without Words*

A rose does not need my words
to contour its petals
with velvet,
to create
the evolution
of its unfolding.

Without words
I might become the rose,
pressing out
from within my
perfumed pores,
intoxicating the air.

## *Trinity*

wing:    one can be enough
　　　　　full and spanned
　　　　　to have your back

prayer:  two hands
　　　　　cupped and empty
　　　　　to hold your hope

faith:    a single word
　　　　　silent
　　　　　invisible

## *Hummingbird*

An exhilaration
of wings
hurls in
suspended motion,
a glimpse of green glitter.

Staccato heartbeats flutter,
a brief blur
in my window.

Her needle-nose beak
still and pointing,
as if to speak,

she darts
into the morning.

## *Without Conclusion*

the sky is without conclusion
open-ended,
beyond where
any star sits

she does not imprison her clouds
but allows white vapors
to billow
and disintegrate

plays host to the winds
which caress a face
or topple the foundation
of anything

the wide-wings
of pelicans drift
through this same
invisible air

who can know
where the sky
ends and
one breath begins

## *Hope Afloat*

Imagine its head
barely above the surface
swiveling and vigilant

waiting
for its ship
weighed down with treasure

or for a small craft
equipped with oars

or even a raft
with rubber handles

no
imagine hope
resting and relieved
no longer waiting
for anything

riding the one wave
that will carry it home

## *A Discarded Tendril*

I plunge the stem
of one green shoot
into grainy potting soil.

It grows
and multiplies,
one root enough
to feed the multitude.

Now the many leaves
wait patiently,
their vines intertwined.

A little water sends them
standing straight up

silent and singing.

## *Liberty*

The chiseled lady holds
her stone torch
and forever calls

Come as you are
always a few minutes behind
with your edges frayed
and threads loose
not yet
tied into neat knots

Come as you are
Still looking
for the lost earring
for the word that says
   what you mean
   what you don't mean
for love in the right places

Come as you are
feeling like you didn't quite arrive
that you can't stay
forgetting why you
came to begin with

Knowing
you cannot know
what happens
until you arrive

## *Stealing Home*

You do not have to have the bases covered
dressed in your flannel knickers, shirt and cap
scooting back and forth like a frantic monkey
spitting tobacco on the mound
now pitching
now catching
stooping in the outfield
wearing a leather mitt

You do not have to have the bases covered
lest that small hard sphere
cracks across the field
or soars out of sight
because you missed the signal
or tripped over your own feet
and marred the manicured dirt

You can stroll off that field

wade
into the meadow
where soft grasses
sway against your skin

## *Hide and Seek*

In my childhood days
I would nestle into cubby holes
closets and corners
in the hope
of not being found

These days
I long to be seen
to be discovered
right where I am

No need to play the chameleon
whose heart is pounding

I want to be
caught in the act
of being myself

I await the words
I see you

My reply
I am here

## *The Offering*

Place them here—
the sticks and stones,
and splintered bones,

the past suns and
slivered moons,
the frail pages
of the books,
now volumes,
packed with old things.

the eighth grade vulgarities,
the merriments of each marriage,
and their dissolutions.

Place them all here—
and watch every scrap
go up in flame,

smoke rising.

## *Home*

nomad that you are

rest
in this oasis

allow
shade
at last

there is a place
to arrive

a cool cloth
for your sweaty brow

breathe deeply
ride your giant exhale

you traveled far
to land
in your own
center

## *Here*

Thank you for all that
is here. Anything else
is too complicated.

## *Dance*

An open heart
folds and unfolds
in the unseen rhythm
of petals,
a rhythm
that transcends time,
like waves
sliding in and out
over and over;
the moon's slivers swelling
to wholeness
again and again.

The rose, invisible,
seeding, sprouting, then
shooting its glaring red
stalk for all its worth
to produce one fragile bud,
and all the while
green leaves everywhere sway
and pelicans skim the sea.

The dance of it,
wild and still
is always here.

# about the author

MARYANN RUSSO is a new voice in American poetry. Her poems have appeared in numerous publications, including *Lunarosity, Sugar Mule, Pace,* and *poeticdiversity*. Maryann's work invites readers to return to the place that has always been within, often using the natural world as a bridge. One of her poems was nominated for the prestigious 2013 Pushcart Prize. She is currently working on her next book of poetry. Maryann is a psychotherapist who lives and works in Redondo Beach, CA.

Visit Maryann at www.Facebook.com/MaryannRussoAuthor and www.OverAndAboveCreative.com

www.ingramcontent.com/pod-product-compliance
Lightning Source LLC
Chambersburg PA
CBHW071743040426
42446CB00012B/2453